PRAISE FOR
7 WAYS TO REDUCE ANXIETY IN 7 MINUTES OR LESS

"Anyone suffering with stress and anxiety will be struggling with two big questions. Firstly "What on earth is happening to me?" and secondly, "What can I do to feel better fast? In this gem of a book, Tony Yuile answers both these questions quite brilliantly. This is a refreshing resource for anyone looking to deal with stress and anxiety in their life. Tony teaches the things that actually work (and work quickly). Fantastic book for anyone seeking real effective help."

- Ed Lester, Founder of the NZ School of Professional Hypnotherapy and NZ Life Coaching

"Because of the very nature of anxiety, if you have it you want simple clear solutions: solutions you can use right now. You also want to know that the person giving them has experience helping people like you, and that their methods are realistic, researched and tested in practical day to day life. The book you are holding gives you all that and more. Tony Yuile has a wealth of experience guiding people from anxiety to calmness. Here are seven immediately usable solutions that he has used himself and shared with so many others in his coaching practice."

- Dr Richard Bolstad, Trainer and author of 14 books including the University text Transforming Communication

7 WAYS TO REDUCE **ANXIETY** IN 7 MINUTES OR LESS

Think clearly, feel relaxed and perform at your best under pressure

Tony Yuile

First published June 2016

Contact: info@tycoaching.nz

Visit our web site at www.tycoaching.nz

ISBN: 978-0-473-35339-1

You may not control all the events that happen to you
but you can decide not to be reduced by them.
– Dr Maya Angelou

I recommend you seek professional help if you need it, but don't underestimate your own ability to take action and make positive, life-changing decisions to help you take back control of your wellbeing.

To Mary, your love, encouragement and support made my transformation possible.

Contents

Introduction

Anxiety is like a rocking chair. It gives you something to do, but it doesn't get you very far.

– Jodi Picoult

This book, although short, is packed with useful information and contains seven proven, practical, easy-to-apply techniques which you can use at any time to minimize the negative impact of day-to-day anxiety.

MY GOALS FOR THIS BOOK

If you've bought this book, you're probably suffering from some degree of anxiety or stress. You are not alone. Everyone experiences anxiety from time to time. It is a natural and inescapable human experience. However, more severe and frequent anxiety in the form of phobias and anxiety disorders for example, can become incapacitating. It's estimated that 10-15% of adults suffer anxiety disorders in their lifetime, females more often than males. The good news is, with the right knowledge and skills you can keep anxiety from dominating your life.

My goals for this book are to provide you with:

a. an understanding of what anxiety is and how we create it; and
b. seven easy-to-apply, effective techniques you can use immediately to start controlling and reducing your day-to-day anxiety.

The seven techniques in this book are taken from the *Fear-Less Coaching Toolbox* I developed and use on a daily basis, to help my clients perform at their best under pressure, reduce stress and master anxiety.

A SOLUTION-FOCUSED APPROACH

My solution-focused approach to helping clients gain control of their anxiety draws on the latest findings from neuroscience and psychology about how we create and maintain anxiety.

THE SEVEN TECHNIQUES

No matter how your anxiety manifests itself, you'll find the seven techniques in this book really helpful in reducing the level of your day-to-day anxiety. These techniques have worked for me and for my clients. Now it's your turn to experience their effectiveness.

Best wishes, Tony

01

What Is Anxiety?

Anxiety is a gift from nature because it aids survival
— none of us would live long if anxiety didn't stop us from taking foolhardy risks!
– Human Givens Institute

The word 'anxiety' is a derivative of the Latin word* angō*, which means 'I cause physical pain' or 'I torment, trouble, vex, distress'.

When first researching anxiety, I soon became confused by the plethora of definitions. Anxiety has been defined as:

- an emotion
- a feeling
- a behavior
- a state of mind
- a consequence of stress
- a cause of stress

After working with anxious and stressed clients for a while, I realised that the majority of people use 'anxiety' and 'stress' as shorthand for the range of symptoms they are experiencing. Therefore, when explaining anxiety to my clients I use the following definition:

'Anxiety' is an umbrella term, used to describe the symptoms produced as a consequence of activating the stress response.

Whenever I refer to 'anxiety' in this book, I'm referring to the symptoms we experience. These symptoms can be found in Chapter 5: How Do We Know We Are Experiencing Anxiety?

THE UPSIDE AND DOWNSIDE OF ANXIETY

Many clients come to me with the goal of becoming completely free of anxiety. That's an unrealistic goal, because the capacity to experience anxiety is innate and of survival value.

Anxiety evolved to protect us from physical harm, and today it also helps us to satisfy our physical and emotional needs. It's an intrinsic part of the human condition. The only people who do not experience anxiety are psychopaths.

So I explain to clients that their goal is to not to eliminate anxiety but to gain control over their anxiety so it serves them (the upside), rather than having a damaging impact on their performance and physical and mental health (the downside).

Now, let's take a look at the two sides of anxiety.

THE UPSIDE OF ANXIETY

Anxiety has always played an important role in keeping humans alive and safe from physical harm, in a world full of uncertainties and risks. It still has an important role to play today, because it's okay to experience a level of fear about things we are uncertain about. Apprehension, unease and nervousness are our early warning system.

These feelings stop us from taking unnecessary risks, and encourage us to be cautious in our actions. Those actions may involve us planning and preparing for threats, e.g. earthquake proofing our house, buying insurance before we go on holiday, rehearsing before delivering a presentation, studying in preparation for an exam.

In particular, we need to experience some level of anxiety when we find ourselves faced with a new or challenging event, a problem, or find ourselves in an unfamiliar or potentially dangerous situation.

When we're faced with an experience we've never had before, it is healthy to have some anxiety because it tells us *"there are things we don't know"* and we have to obtain more information, skills or resources. For example, without anxiety (over the fear of failure) we wouldn't prepare for the job interview we have next week.

A certain amount of anxiety enhances our performance when we are faced with something challenging. Professional speakers, actors, athletes and other performers consistently rely on the heightened arousal of nervousness to channel extra energy into their performance. A reasonable level of nervousness before an interview or exam, for example, is likely to result in better preparation and, therefore, a better result.

When we are faced with a problem, a certain amount of anxiety can be a good thing because it makes use of that most powerful of human assets – the imagination – to consider various scenarios and options before arriving at the best possible solution.

The anxiety we may feel in unfamiliar surroundings, e.g. while walking near steep cliffs, will cause us to be more careful and purposeful in our movements.

Crossing a road is an example of a potentially dangerous situation. Without anxiety (over the fear of being knocked down), we wouldn't be careful as we crossed.

THE DOWNSIDE OF ANXIETY

While anxiety has ensured our survival as a species – helping us survive physical, life-threatening dangers – in today's world it can be problematic because the majority of the dangers and threats we face are not physical or life threatening. Today the main cause of anxiety is the misuse of our imagination. We create negative future scenarios in the virtual reality machine that is our imagination. Basically, we scare ourselves with threats that are unlikely to materialise into real dangers. When our fears are irrational or unreal they can prevent us from taking the action we need to take, and this can have a negative impact on our lives – perhaps to the point where we become dysfunctional.

From a behavioural perspective, avoidance is the main downside of anxiety. When experiencing anxiety we may avoid both familiar and new experiences.

Stepping outside of our comfort zone is often avoided. [The comfort zone is a behavioral state within which an individual operates in an anxiety-neutral condition, using a limited set of behaviors to deliver a steady level of performance, usually without a sense of risk.] So we play safe, and do not pursue opportunities or we avoid new experiences.

Avoiding experiences we used to enjoy is common.

Failing to take necessary action is a form of avoidance. We engage in procrastination, perfectionism and 'paralysis by analysis'. Paralysis by analysis occurs when we over-analyze (or over-think) a situation so a decision or action is never taken, in effect paralyzing the outcome.

02

How We Create Anxiety

Men are disturbed not by things, but by the view which they take of them.

– Epictetus, Greek Philosopher circa 100AD

This is the process by which we create anxiety:

A Specific Context

Information is received through our senses

We perceive what the sensory information means

The meaning generates an emotion

If the Meaning = Threat Or Danger
&
The Emotion = Fear

Then .....

The Stress Response is activated

The Stress Response produces ANXIETY

LET'S EXPLORE EACH OF THE STEPS IN THIS PROCESS.

STEP 1: A Specific Context

This is the specific environment, situation, object or person that provides us with sensory information. Some examples of everyday specific contexts include being stuck in a traffic jam; attending a job interview; watching a TV program; having an argument with our partner; watching or participating in a sporting competition; walking into a room full of strangers; reading about an increase in mortgage interest rates. The possibilities are endless.

STEP 2: Information is Received Through our Senses

Sensory information is received from:

a) the external environment; and/or
b) our internal environment – i.e. bodily sensations (such as aches and pains), feelings (such as sadness), thoughts (about the past, the present and the future).

Here's an interesting and important fact - our mind can't tell the difference between something that's real and something that's vividly imagined.

STEP 3: We Perceive what the Sensory Information Means

Perception is the process of recognizing and interpreting the sensory information we receive. In this way, we are able to understand and react to the world around us.

We create meaning and make sense of the world by matching sensory information to our innate knowledge, memories, beliefs, emotional needs and values. This process is called 'pattern matching'.

Because each of us has a unique set of memories, beliefs, emotional needs and values, our interpretation is, in turn, unique to us. This means a situation one person perceives as a threat, might, to the next person, be perceived as a challenge. It's why two witnesses to the same incident often provide different accounts of what happened.

The human brain has evolved to help ensure our survival in a world full of danger. Its main job was (and still is) to look out for anything that could kill or harm us and avoid it, or if we couldn't avoid it, fight for our lives. So the first stage in the pattern-matching process is to determine if the environment poses a threat to our continued physical and/or emotional survival.

This 'threat detection' happens in the brain's early warning center – the amygdala, which forms a part of the limbic system (the emotional brain). The amygdala helps to store memories of events and emotions so we are able to recognize similar events in the future. It remembers the things that are dangerous and/or could stop us from meeting our physical and emotional needs.

Pattern matching by the amygdala is essential but it is by necessity a sloppy process because our survival depends on our being able to respond quickly to real or potential danger. Sloppy or faulty pattern matching often results in us experiencing fear when we don't need to, in response to something that isn't really threatening. Faulty pattern matches are at the heart of all psychological problems including anxiety.

If the amygdala identifies a threat, it immediately sounds the alarm which activates the stress response and our body prepares for action. A rush of stress hormones floods the body and the emotional brain overwhelms ('hijacks') the prefrontal cortex (our thinking brain.). This inhibits our working memory and is why, when the stress response is triggered, we are unable to think clearly and rationally. All of this activity happens outside of conscious awareness.

Provided the amygdala doesn't sound the alarm, the pre-frontal cortex analyses the information and determines a meaning. For example, every word you are currently reading is being pattern matched in your mind to an association you have with the word so you can create meaning from what you read.

STEP 4: THE MEANING GENERATES AN EMOTION

We react to the meaning by generating an emotion. In the case of a threat, the emotion we experience is fear.

How much fear we experience is mostly determined by the non-conscious (out of awareness) appraisal we make concerning how:

- prepared we are to cope with the threat
- much control we believe we have over the threat
- severe the physical and/or emotional impact will be, if the threat materializes

In order to experience anxiety and stress, we must believe at some level that we are unable to cope effectively with the (present or future) situation with the resources we have at our disposal. When we believe we have adequate resources to cope with a situation then we may perceive the situation as benign or as a challenge. It is our appraisal of the situation as a threat, rather than the objective reality of the threat, that determines how much fear we experience.

The intensity of our fear can range from a vague sense of apprehension and unease through to sheer terror.

For example, there is an angry wasp buzzing around your face. You appraise that:

- the likelihood of the wasp stinging you is high; and
- you can't avoid the wasp; and
- you don't have anything with which to kill or ward off the wasp; and
- a sting will be very painful.

As a result of this non-conscious appraisal, you experience fear verging on panic.

Fear instantly mobilizes our sympathetic nervous system and activates the stress response which prepares our body and mind for action to either avoid or to deal with the threat.

STEP 5: THE STRESS RESPONSE IS ACTIVATED

The stress response is commonly referred to as the 'fight or flight' response.

As mentioned earlier, when faced with a threat – real or imagined – we react quickly ('leaping before we look') rather than waste time, consciously assessing the threat. Every millisecond counts when our survival is at stake.

Once the stress response is activated, our emotional brain 'hijacks' the pre-frontal cortex, locking us into black and white thinking. This means access is restricted to the logical, rational centers in the pre-frontal cortex, and our working memory is reduced (the memory we need for thinking). It then becomes almost impossible for us to think clearly and rationally and consider alternatives. As far as our emotional brain is concerned, we can't be worrying about the finer details when a lifesaving decision on how to avoid or escape the threat has to be made. We need a quick decision – do we fight or take flight?

STEP 6: THE STRESS RESPONSE PRODUCES ANXIETY

The fight or flight response produces the mental and physiological symptoms we associate with anxiety, e.g. altered perceptions, 'butterflies' in the stomach, sweating, rapid breathing.

The more intense the fear, the more intense and numerous the symptoms may be. Sheer terror will elicit more severe symptoms than those triggered by mild apprehension.

Once we experience the symptoms, those symptoms may themselves become the stimulus for a new cycle of the process. In this way, we can quickly get caught in an anxiety loop, a self-perpetuating cycle in which the process repeats itself over and over. Each repetition ramps up the intensity and duration of the symptoms. For some people, this may result in a panic attack, or if the symptoms persist over a period of time they may generalize into an anxiety disorder.

Once we perceive the threat is over, or has been dealt with, the symptoms dissipate as our mind/body system rebalances itself.

Here's a simple example of how we might experience anxiety:

THE SITUATION	THE STEP IN THE PROCESS
John is sitting in reception at ABC Ltd, waiting to go into an interview for his dream job.	**A specific context**
The door to the interview room opens, and an ashen-faced interviewee emerges.	**External sensory information**
John's mind conjures up a scenario in which he's being grilled by the interview panel. He sees himself struggling to answer even the easiest of their questions.	**Internal sensory information**
John's amygdala pattern matches this imagined scenario to an extremely uncomfortable interview he experienced early in his career when he had a complete 'meltdown'.	**Meaning = threat**
John experiences an intense sense of impending doom.	**Emotional arousal**
	Stress response activated
In an instant, John's heart rate increases, he feels nauseous and he has a sudden compelling desire to flee the building.	**Anxiety is experienced**

03

What's The Difference Between Anxiety And Stress?

Anxiety is nothing but repeatedly re-experiencing failure in advance. What a waste.

– Seth Godin, Author

I'm often asked, "What's the difference between anxiety and stress?"

The answer, based on my definition of anxiety, is: **"there is no significant difference."** 'Anxiety' and 'stress' are just different words we use to describe the symptoms produced by the stress response.

There is, however, a difference in:

How anxiety and stress are created:

ANXIETY: The trigger is an imagined threat: in a few days' time, you have to make a presentation to a group of colleagues and you imagine you are going to perform badly and make a fool of yourself.

STRESS: The trigger is an external, real and immediate danger: you have begun your presentation to a group of colleagues and PowerPoint crashes.

How long the symptoms persist:

ANXIETY: The flight or fight response will continue to be activated for as long as we continue to imagine the threat. For example, chronic worrying will maintain the symptoms.

STRESS: Once we've dealt with the immediate danger, and provided we are unharmed, the symptoms dissipate as our mind/body returns to its normal balanced steady-state.

It's often the case that we experience stress followed by anxiety. For example:

It's Friday. You have begun your presentation to a group of colleagues and PowerPoint crashes. Your amygdala sounds the alarm, the stress response is activated and you experience stress: your mind goes blank, you start to sweat, and you feel a rising sense of panic. You can't get PowerPoint to work so you cancel the presentation.

As you walk off stage, your imagination is already creating a scenario in which your colleagues are mocking you and complaining about how you wasted their time. In this imagined scenario, your boss is waiting at your desk looking like he's a volcano about to blow its top.

The stress response is activated again and you now experience anxiety: you feel a sense of dread; you begin asking yourself 'what if' questions; you feel nauseous and have an incredible urge to go home. So you tell a colleague you're feeling unwell and you leave.

Now you are experiencing anxiety everything in your surroundings becomes a potential threat. You spend the weekend jumpy and agitated. Since the stress response diverts blood and resources away from your digestive tract, you lose your appetite. Your adrenalin is pumping, so you don't sleep much. By Monday morning, you are tired, angry and go into work ready to verbally attack anyone who criticizes or mocks you about Friday's cancelled presentation.

04

Changing The Way You Create Anxiety To Get A Different Outcome

The greatest weapon against stress is our ability to choose one thought over another.

– William James, Philosopher and Psychologist

WHEN YOU CHANGE THE WAY YOU CREATE ANXIETY, YOU GET A DIFFERENT OUTCOME

We've seen that anxiety doesn't just descend out of nowhere; we create our day-to-day anxiety through the misuse of our imagination. This understanding is empowering. It provides us with a blueprint for how to control our anxiety and allows us to be proactive in managing it rather than just being passively reactive.

The really good news is that we have plenty of opportunities to intervene in the anxiety creation process and, in doing so, change the outcome. Let's take a look at the first three steps in the process and some of the possible beneficial actions we might take.

Step 1: CONTEXT - Possible Beneficial Actions:

When you change, or avoid, a specific environment (the context) you change the sensory information you receive. Here are some examples of how you might change your environment:

- find a new employer/become your own boss
- work from home
- take a less congested route to work
- turn off the TV news and reality programs
- get rid of the clutter clogging up your working/living space
- avoid pessimistic, energy-sapping people
- remove caffeine, sugar and processed foods from your diet.

Step 2: SENSORY INFORMATION - Possible Beneficial Actions:

When we change the sensory information we receive, we change our perception and understanding of the world around us.

In addition to the sensory information we receive from our environment, a key source of information is our self-talk. What many people don't realize is that anxiety is really hard to create without self-talk (internal dialogue). We are constantly talking to ourselves. It's estimated we have 60,000 - 70,000 thoughts a day and about 90% of those thoughts are negative, i.e. potentially anxiety inducing!

When you get into the habit of paying attention to your internal dialogue – noticing the commentary or thoughts passing through your mind – you will begin to realize just how much it influences your perception.

Having developed the ability to pay attention to your internal dialogue, you will be in a position to spot and challenge negative messages. You can then replace those messages with positive, more empowering, optimistic and life-enhancing ones.

Step 3: PERCEPTION - Possible Beneficial Actions:

When you change your pattern-matching templates, or 'mental filters' (i.e. beliefs, values, attitudes, assumptions about the world), you change the meaning you give to an experience – real or imagined.

In her book, *The Upside of Stress: Why Stress Is Good for You, and How to Get Good at It (2015),* Kelly McGonigal describes how simply reframing a situation as a challenge rather than a threat can result in a person feeling a sense of excitement rather than anxiety and stress.

CHANGE THE DURATION AND INTENSITY OF SOME OR ALL OF YOUR SYMPTOMS

Another option available to us is to change the duration and intensity of some or all of our symptoms. A great way to do this is through deep relaxation. The fact is you can't be anxious and relaxed at the same time. That's why the first of the seven techniques in this book is a relaxation exercise (7-11 breathing). However, as you'll discover, each of the seven techniques will help you to dissipate your anxiety.

05

How Do We Know We Are Experiencing Anxiety?

If we are honest with ourselves, most of us will have to admit that we live our lives on an ocean of fear.

– Jon Kabat-Zinn

You may not know you are experiencing anxiety because, anxiety manifests in so many different ways, involving a wide range of symptoms. Plus we can get so used to the symptoms that they just become the accepted norm for us.

Because the mind and body are one system, anxiety symptoms appear in the form of cognitive (mental), emotional, physiological (physical changes) and behavioral (observable actions) responses. Some people may experience anxiety as a combination of all these responses at the same time.

Let's take a closer look at what we could expect to experience in each of the four categories of symptom.

Cognitive
➢ Repetitive thinking (with a fixed view of a situation that may bear little or no relation to reality) ➢ Forgetful ➢ Hyper vigilance ➢ Poor concentration/focus ➢ 'What if?' thinking ➢ Catastrophizing ➢ Black and white thinking ➢ Worrying

Emotional

- Anticipation
- Apprehension
- Distress
- Dread, sense of danger or impending doom
- Fear or terror
- Feeling overwhelmed
- Jumpiness or edginess
- Nervousness
- Panic
- Uneasiness

Physiological

- A feeling of restlessness
- Feeling 'keyed up' or 'on-edge'
- Rapid heartbeat, palpitations
- Excessive perspiration
- Cold or sweaty palms, feeling cold or overheated
- Numbness or tingling in the hands
- Shortness of breath
- Rapid breathing, hyperventilating
- Trembling, dizziness, weakness
- Muscle tension,
- 'Butterflies' in the stomach
- Chest pain
- Nausea
- Fatigue, tiredness
- Indigestion

Behavioral

- **Attack/Defend (Fight):** We may verbally or physically attack someone. We may be irritable. We may be desperate to bring the situation to an end. Because we are on alert, we may find it difficult to relax or sleep.

- **Avoid/Withdraw/Escape (Flight):** We may:
  - withdraw or avoid situations that we know make us afraid.
  - begin to make excuses and start to avoid things and situations that we associate with our anxiety.
  - flee places or situations where we feel fear.

  This avoidance behavior eventually narrows the scope of our life as we opt for the safety of routine and sameness.

- **Freeze:** We may procrastinate or engage in paralysis by analysis. Our mind goes blank just when we need information. We may experience lethargy.

06

Anxiety Disorders

I'm a bundle of nerves riddled with irrational fears.
– Tori Spelling, Actress

As we've learnt, some level of anxiety is normal and, for the most part, beneficial. How can we tell if our day-to-day anxiety has crossed the line into a disorder? The distinction between an anxiety disorder and just having normal brief anxiety is that an anxiety disorder:

- occurs more often and more intensely
- seems to happen without reason
- is out of proportion to the real or imagined threat
- persists, often for months
- becomes a constant and dominating force that severely disrupts the quality and enjoyment of our everyday life.

There are many types of anxiety disorder, and each one can become as disabling as any chronic physical illness, interfering with a normal lifestyle. The two most common forms of anxiety disorder people experience are social anxiety and generalized (free floating) anxiety.

Excessive anxiety clouds our thinking, causes emotional pain and distress and can lead to physical illness. In short, it drains the joy from life.

HOW PREVALENT ARE ANXIETY DISORDERS?

Millions of people worldwide experience an anxiety disorder. It's estimated one in four people in New Zealand will experience an anxiety disorder to one degree or another in their lifetime. Of those many thousands of people, just 30 percent of cases will be diagnosed, and only five percent will seek professional help.

THE MAIN FORMS OF ANXIETY DISORDER AND THEIR SYMPTOMS

Anxiety disorders manifest in many different ways involving a wide range of symptoms. Some symptoms are unique to the type of anxiety disorder or to the individual. The table below describes the main forms of anxiety disorder and their symptoms.

ANXIETY DISORDER	SYMPTOMS
Generalized Anxiety Disorder (Free Floating)	Constant worry and chronic apprehension, disproportionate to situations, leading to headaches, nausea, sleep problems, digestive problems, sweating.
Obsessive Compulsive Disorder (OCD)	Recurrent, unwanted thoughts (obsessions) and/or repetitive behaviours (compulsions) such as checking, washing etc.
Panic Disorder	Repeated attacks of intense fear, palpitations, sweating, vomiting or diarrhoea, feeling faint/dizzy. The person lives in fear that another attack will occur.
Post-Traumatic Stress Disorder (PTSD)	Can occur after a traumatic event. The person re-experiences the trauma in dreams, flashbacks and memories. They may experience emotional numbing, avoidance, panic attacks, insomnia.
Specific Phobias (including Social Anxiety Disorder)	Irrational, intense and persistent fear of certain situations, activities, things, animals, or people. The person may be hypervigilant.

Treating Anxiety Disorders

The treatment of an anxiety disorder may involve therapy or medication or a combination of both. The good news is that for the majority of people treatment works!

Important: The techniques in this book will help you to control the symptoms of day-to-day anxiety, triggered in response to specific threats. They are not the solution for an anxiety disorder. Advice on the treatment of anxiety disorders is outside the scope of this book. If you believe you have an anxiety disorder I recommend you consult your doctor or a medical professional in the first instance.

07

Sometimes We Just Want Quick, Simple, Effective Relief

He who is not every day conquering some fear
has not learned the secret of life.
– Shannon L Alder, Author

Here are seven easy-to-apply, quick to take effect, proven techniques for reducing day-to-day anxiety. Each technique takes less than seven minutes to perform. I recommend you practice all seven, then when you are feeling the onset of anxiety, simply pick the one(s) that work best for you.

TECHNIQUE 1:
Breathe Away Anxiety

TECHNIQUE 2:
Be A*W*A*R*E of your Anxiety

TECHNIQUE 3:
Your Calm Anchor

TECHNIQUE 4:
Clench Your Left Fist for 30 Seconds

TECHNIQUE 5:
Spin Anxiety Away

TECHNIQUE 6:
Passing a Ball from Hand to Hand

TECHNIQUE 7:
Heart-Centered Breathing

TECHNIQUE 1: Breathe Away Anxiety

FACT - the stress response cannot remain activated if the body's natural relaxation response (part of our parasympathetic nervous system) is activated. Either the stress response is activated or the relaxation response is activated. So when we know how to activate our relaxation response, we can switch off the stress response and enjoy the significant physical and psychological benefits of being able to relax and calm down.

The first thing I teach my anxious clients is a simple, reliable, pleasant way to relax that just involves breathing. It's called 7-11 breathing and it's easy to learn, only takes two or three minutes to do, you can do it anywhere (in bed, on a bus or the train, even whilst walking gently), and best of all, you begin to experience the benefits almost immediately.

THE TECHNIQUE

1. Keep your shoulders down and breathe through the nose slowly, deeply and evenly from the diaphragm, i.e. your tummy moves in and out as if it had a balloon inflating when you breathe in, and deflating as you breathe out. Some people find it helpful to put their hand on their tummy to feel it inflating like a balloon, as this lets them know they're doing it right.

2. Breathe in for a count of 7, counting the numbers to yourself in your head.

3. Breathe out, at the same pace as the in breath, for a count of 11, counting the numbers to yourself in your head. You may find you have to breathe in slightly 'harder' and breathe out 'more gently' to prevent having to gasp for air!

4. The secret to the effectiveness of this technique is to make each out breath last longer than each in breath – hence 7-11. This has the effect of stimulating the parasympathetic nervous system. By changing your pattern of breathing in this way, your body automatically begins to relax.

5. If you find you are unable to breathe out for a count of 11, hold your breath for the remainder of the time while you keep counting to 11 and then breathe in again. Alternatively, you can breathe in to the count of 3 and out, more slowly, to the count of 5. Remember, the important thing is to make each exhale last longer than each inhale without getting out of breath!

6. Breathe like this for between 10 and 20 breaths, noticing how you relax more and more with each breath.

7. Concentrate on the counting (if your mind wanders off, just gently bring it back to the count) and feel the welcome sense of calm gradually flowing in. Counting also has the effect of distracting your mind and your mind can't be worrying or analyzing things at the same time as counting.

8. Get a sense of how much less tense you start to feel, just by breathing in this way and by distracting your mind you can let go of any negative thoughts and worries.

FOR AN EVEN BETTER EFFECT, ENGAGE YOUR IMAGINATION

It can really help to deepen the sense of relaxation if you can imagine yourself in a place which feels safe and calm while you practice your 7-11 breathing. Some people imagine being on a warm beach, some a tranquil garden, others by a gentle stream or walking in a wood or in the hills. Others prefer to imagine being curled up in their bed.

Wherever you choose to be in your imagination, engage all your senses into creating this imaginary place with its sights, colors, sounds, feelings (e.g. sun on your skin), tastes or smells. Using all your senses in this way, even though just pretending, can really help your body and mind to relax because, as mentioned earlier, our mind can't tell the difference between something real and something vividly imagined.

TECHNIQUE 2:
Be A*W*A*R*E Of Your Anxiety

The key to reducing your anxiety is to accept it completely. Fighting it only stimulates the stress response even more. The A*W*A*R*E technique is an effective cognitive behavioral technique for reducing anxiety that involves accepting the feelings of anxiety and then becoming detached from them.

1. ACCEPT THE ANXIETY

When you feel anxious, acknowledge that your brain is simply trying to help you in the best way it knows how. Accept that you're responding to a false alarm and accept the emotions and feelings. Do not fight them or try to wish them away. The more you are willing to face them, the less intense they will become. Wait, and give the feelings time to pass without resisting them. Telling yourself *"Don't panic!"*, for example, only makes things worse because when we resist something, it has a tendency to persist.

It's important to note that you are not accepting the cause of the anxiety, and you are not giving in to the anxiety. This acceptance step is simply about acknowledging your anxiety, not resisting it, just allowing it to be present. Once you accept the anxiety you can begin to transform it.

2. WATCH YOUR ANXIETY

Stay in the present. Remember you are not your anxiety; it's the result of a mind/body process. Simply notice, without judgement, what you are thinking, feeling, sensing. You might feel overwhelmed, fearful, distressed, a sense of panic, etc.

Be detached from the anxiety and notice what is really happening to you, as opposed to what you think 'might' happen. If you find yourself asking *"What if?"* tell yourself *"So what!"*

Now say out loud what you are noticing: *"I'm feeling _______."*

When you watch and acknowledge anxiety like this, it will naturally start to dissipate.

As you wait for the feelings to dissipate, tell yourself, with real intention, one or more of these statements (or something similar):

"Thank you for trying to alert me and help me, but you've misread the situation. I'm perfectly safe."

"You're a false message from my brain and I'm choosing to ignore you."

"This is just a sign that my nervous system is working normally. The feelings will pass."

"I'm no longer going to fight you anxiety. I'm allowing you to be here. I accept and allow these anxious feelings."

As you continue to watch your anxiety, sense it changing into a different feeling, and perhaps say to yourself, *"I accept and allow this new feeling."*

Remember, although your symptoms may be unpleasant and frightening, they are not dangerous or harmful. If you've read Chapter 2: How We Create Anxiety, you will now understand that what you are experiencing is just your body's response to a faulty pattern match. It's simply a false alarm.

3. ACT WITH THE ANXIETY

Continue to behave normally, doing what you intended to do. Use 7-11 breathing (see Technique 1) to calm yourself. Sometimes this is enough on its own. If you avoid or run from the situation, your anxiety will reduce temporarily but will return, and probably at a higher level. When you act with the anxiety, you de-condition yourself to its impact.

If you find yourself thinking about the anxiety triggering event, person or thing, distract yourself by focusing on and carrying out a simple and manageable task such as counting backwards from 100 by 3s or clicking your fingers.

Give yourself some supportive, present tense, positive, progressive affirmatio. Preferably say them out loud. The affirmations could be ones you create for yourself, or you may prefer to use one of the examples below:

"I am becoming calmer and more and more relaxed with each and every breath."

"I am getting better and better at handling this feeling – and remaining calm and relaxed."

"This feeling of ____________(e.g. anxiety/ stress/ overwhelm/ panic) is beginning to pass."

"I am getting better and better at handling whatever I am feeling."

"I accept this feeling and choose to let it go."

You can use your affirmation(s) throughout the day, or whenever you notice you are beginning to feel anxiety building.

REPEAT STEPS 1 TO 3

Continue to accept your anxiety, watching it and acting with it until it falls to a comfortable level.

EXPECT THE BEST

Anxiety is the end result of our misusing our imagination to create fearful future scenarios. Remember what you fear most may never happen. Why not surprise yourself the next time you feel anxious, by the effective way in which you handle it, simply by being more A*W*A*R*E

Adapted from: *Anxiety Disorders and Phobias: A Cognitive Perspective*, Beck, Emery and Greenberg (1985)

TECHNIQUE 3: Your Calm Anchor

An anchor is simply a conditioned response, also called a conditioned reflex.

Anchoring refers to the creation of an anchor through associating a feeling with a sensory experience, such as a touch or a sound. This association is formed when neurons in the brain physically wire themselves together as actions are repeated simultaneously enough times and/or with enough intensity. (The expression "neurons that fire together wire together" was coined by Canadian psychologist Donald Hebb half a century ago.)

We form natural associations between feelings and external sights, sounds, smells, tastes, and sensations, every day – whether we intend to or not. Every day our anchors remind us of those feelings. Very often we are totally unaware of the anchor, and we are baffled as to why we suddenly feel happy, sad, afraid, or some other emotion. For example, a smell may instantly transport us back to a particular time, a song may bring back memories of a person long gone, and a particular image may trigger feelings of fear or happiness.

We can use this natural ability to create anchors, to design and install a 'calm anchor'. Later when we trigger our calm anchor we instantly experience a calm, relaxed state of mind and physiology.

CREATING AN ANCHOR

There are four simple rules to follow when you create an anchor.

1. **STATE INTENSITY.** You must be experiencing the calm, relaxed feelings intensely.

2. **PRECISE TIMING**. You must time the creation of the anchor to happen while you are experiencing this intense state, not before or after it.

3. **UNIQUENESS.** The action by which the anchor is created and triggered must be something that is not going to happen by accident at other times. Two possible options I suggest to my clients are: squeezing the thumb and ring finger of their non-dominant hand together or lightly squeezing an earlobe between the thumb and forefinger.

4. **REPLICABLE.** The action must be something you can repeat in exactly the same way (including the same amount of pressure), whenever you want to recreate the feeling of calm and relaxation.

CREATING YOUR CALM ANCHOR

1. Get comfortable. Make sure you won't be disturbed. Sit or lie down in a comfortable place and close your eyes. Last thing at night or first thing in the morning when you're in bed can be great times to set an anchor as your mind is more likely to be open and receptive. Use 7-11 breathing to trigger a nice, calm, relaxed state.
2. Now build on this sense of relaxation by remembering a specific time when you felt really, really calm, relaxed and in control. Fully return to it now and imagine being in your body at that time, seeing what you saw, hearing what you heard and feeling how good you felt. (If you can't remember a specific time, imagine, pretend or visualize how wonderful it would feel to be totally calm, relaxed and in control – if you had all the ease, comfort and self-control you could ever need).
3. Use as many of your five senses as possible to make this specific time as vivid and real as possible. Then imagine stepping into this memory/visualization, and as you experience it, really allow the feelings to build. As you continue to experience this memory/visualization, make the colors brighter and richer, the sounds crisper and the good feelings stronger.

4. Feel yourself becoming more and more calm, relaxed and in control. When you are fairly sure you have almost peaked and couldn't be any more calm and relaxed, set the anchor by squeezing the thumb and ring finger of your non-dominant hand together. By doing this, you are associating this specific movement of your fingers and the specific degree of pressure, with this particular state of calm, relaxed, control.

5. Keep squeezing for 5 to 10 seconds and then separate your thumb and finger and open your eyes. Look around and notice something about the room you're in. Doing this will ensure you have a fresh start each time you set the anchor.

6. Now close your eyes and repeat steps 2, 3 and 4 again.

Go through steps 2, 3 and 4 at least five more times to really lock in these good calm, relaxing, in-control feelings into your neurology. You can use the same specific memory/visualization each time you repeat the steps or use a different calming, relaxing memory/visualization each time. You will know you have repeated the exercise enough times when all you need to do is squeeze your ring finger and thumb together and you can instantly sense those good feelings of calm, relaxation and control spreading through your body.

Note: To get an anchor to set properly, you have to be committed and prepared to repeat the exercise as many times as it takes until the anchor triggers the desired feelings. Because anchoring is a natural process that you are skilled at, you cannot possibly fail to create a calm anchor provided you follow the above steps correctly.

Now, think about a situation you are anxious about. As you start to feel anxious, squeeze your thumb and ring finger together (replicating the action exactly as you did it when setting the anchor) and feel the calm, relaxed feeling spreading through your body and notice how this good feeling replaces any anxious feelings. Notice the difference from only a few minutes ago. Notice how much more in control you feel. Now imagine things going perfectly in that future situation, going exactly as you want them to, and feel how good it feels to be much calmer, relaxed and in control of the situation.

MAINTAINING THE INTENSITY OF YOUR CALM ANCHOR

Anchors can wane in intensity over time. Therefore, make sure you repeat the above exercise regularly to maintain and reinforce the power of your calm anchor.

TECHNIQUE 4:
Clench Your Left Fist For 30 Seconds

In 2012, experts from the Technical University of Munich in Germany discovered that athletes were less likely to buckle under pressure when, before a competition, they squeezed a ball in their left hand rather than their right hand. The experiments involved soccer players, judo experts and badminton players.

Although the researchers aren't sure why, they theorize it is likely because of the way the brain is structured. Previous studies have shown that conscious rumination or anxious thinking, which is controlled by the left side of the brain, can often hamper athletic performance. The right side of the brain has more control over highly-practiced, skilled, automatic performance which is what we rely on under pressure and, importantly, controls movements on the left side of the body.

In other words, by squeezing a ball in your left hand or even just clenching your left fist, you may activate the part of your brain responsible for the body's ability to put aside anxious thought and, as the Nike slogan encourages us – '*Just Do It.*'

So the next time you are under pressure simply clench your left fist. Simply curl your left hand tight into a fist and hold it for 30 seconds. At the same time repeat an affirmation, preferably out loud, telling yourself you are becoming calmer and more relaxed (see Technique 2: Be A*W*A*R*E of Your Anxiety, for some examples of affirmations you might choose to use).

Reference:

1. *Preventing Motor Skill Failure Through Hemisphere-Specific Priming: Cases From Choking Under Pressure*, Juergen Beckmann, Ph.D., Peter Groepel, Ph.D., and Felix Ehrlenspiel, Ph.D., Technical University of Munich; Journal of Experimental Psychology: Sept. 3, 2012.

TECHNIQUE 5:
Spin Anxiety Away

One of the consistent things about anxiety is that it encompasses a physical sensation in the body. This sensation is always moving, and usually it's moving fast. People often describe it as a rushing sensation like an electrical current or a tidal wave through their body. The sensation usually has a temperature associated with it, ranging from white hot to icy cold. This sensation usually moves up or down the body but it doesn't exit the body. It just keeps circulating through the body. This is why we can say anxiety has a spin.

This technique is really simple and fun to do. As well as using it to quickly relieve your own anxiety you can guide family and friends through the process and help them feel less anxious too.

THE TECHNIQUE

1. Close your eyes so you can attend more completely to your feelings. Think about an anxiety-producing situation, and as you do, notice where you first notice the anxiety, triggered by this thought, physically in your body.

2. Now rate this feeling on a scale from 1 to 10, where 10 is unbearable.

3. Now gesture with your hand or fingers to indicate where the feeling is and where the feeling moves to. Doing this gives you a sense of the overall path of the movement of the feeling in your body. Does the feeling spin in a clockwise or counter-clockwise direction along this path?

4. Now imagine moving the spinning feeling outside of your body, and once you feel or sense it outside of yourself, reverse the spin. Notice what changes when you begin to spin that feeling in the opposite direction. (Typically people find the feeling becomes much less intense.)

5. Now give this spinning feeling a color, one that you find relaxing and spin the feeling a bit faster in that (opposite) direction. As you do so, notice what else begins to change.

6. Now imagine bringing the spinning, colored feeling back inside your body, still rotating in the opposite direction. Notice what changes when you spin that feeling, in that (opposite) direction, back inside your body.

7. Now think of something funny, and add some laughter into the spinning, colored feeling.

8. Now re-assess the intensity of the feeling on a scale of 1 to 10. Notice how much lower the intensity is now.

9. Repeat steps 1 - 7 until the level of anxiety has reduced to a level you are comfortable with or it has disappeared.

TECHNIQUE 6: Passing A Ball From Hand To Hand

This simple and effective technique uses visual bilateral stimulation.

Bilateral stimulation is stimuli (visual, auditory or tactile) which occur in a rhythmic left to right pattern. For example, visual bilateral stimulation could involve watching a hand or moving light alternating from left to right and back again. Auditory bilateral stimulation could involve listening to tones that alternate between the left and right sides of the head.

Bilateral stimulation enables us to reprocess memories and patterns of thinking that are disturbing, thus reducing or eliminating their negative impact. So when we deliberately focus on an anxiety-producing thought or memory, and then concentrate on performing bilateral stimulation, our anxiety is reduced. Moreover, the anxiety-producing thought or distressing memory seems to become less distressing in a long-term way.

Visual bilateral stimulation is used in Eye Movement Desensitization and Reprocessing (EMDR) an integrative psychotherapy approach developed by Francine Shapiro. EMDR has been extensively researched and considered effective for the treatment of anxiety disorders, particularly Post-Traumatic Stress Disorder (PTSD).

BILATERAL STIMULATION CREATES FOUR MAIN EFFECTS

1. A relaxation effect, including decreased physiological arousal.
2. Increased attentional flexibility (meaning your thoughts become less 'stuck' on whatever was bothering you).
3. Distancing effect (meaning the problem seems smaller and further away).
4. A reduced level of anxiety.

THE TECHNIQUE

1. Take a ball (or anything small and light that you can pass from hand to hand).
2. Now think of something that is causing you some anxiety.
3. As you think about that thing, notice where in your body you sense the anxiety.
4. As you connect with that sensation, rate the level of that anxiety on a scale of 1 to 10, where 10 is unbearable.
5. As you continue to think about the anxiety triggering situation, begin passing the ball back and forth, starting with the left hand. For best effect move the hand holding the ball across the mid-line of your body and allow the other hand which takes the ball to swing out to the side each time you pass the ball. *This action stimulates both sides of the brain.*
6. Do this for a minute. Stop. Take a deep breath and check in with your body.
7. Now, think about that same anxiety producing situation again and re-rate the level of anxiety. You might find it has already reduced or even dissipated.
8. As you continue to think about the anxiety triggering situation begin passing the ball back and forth again, starting from the left hand.
9. Do this for a minute. Stop. Take a deep breath and check in with your body.
10. Now, think about that same anxiety producing situation again and re-rate the level of anxiety. You might find it has reduced even more or even dissipated.
11. Repeat the process until the level of anxiety has reduced to a level you are comfortable with or has disappeared.

Remember whenever you start to feel anxiety rising, pick up an object, – e.g. a ball, PC mouse, bottle of water, a pen – and start passing the object from your left hand to your right hand, making sure the object crosses the mid-line of your body and allowing the hand which accepts the object to swing out to the side.

The really great thing about this technique is that it's another one you can do anytime and anywhere.

TECHNIQUE 7: Heart-Centered Breathing

This technique helps to reduce anxiety and stress in the moment. It is based on The Quick Coherence ® Technique developed by the HeartMath Institute (HMI). For over two decades, the HMI has been researching heart-brain communication and its relationship to managing stress, increasing coherence and deepening our connection to self and others.

Coherence is a specific physiological state associated with positive emotions, improved physiological functioning, emotional stability and cognitive performance. When you are in a coherent state, your thoughts and emotions are balanced and you experience ease and inner harmony.

THE TECHNIQUE

1. **HEART FOCUS:** After a few relaxing breaths, bring your awareness to your heart or the area of the heart. Keep your focus on the heart area while gently breathing – five seconds in and five seconds out. As you breathe naturally and easily imagine your breath is flowing in and out through the heart area. Repeat this breathing cycle two or three times before moving on to the next step. You might want to hold your hand over your heart, to keep your awareness there, as you imagine breathing through your heart area.

2. **HEART FEELING:** Activate and sustain a genuine feeling of appreciation or care for someone or something in your life. Focus on this good feeling as you continue to breathe through the area of your heart. Imagine breathing these wonderful, positive feelings into your heart, and breathe them out through your heart.

   A variation on this is to include a soothing word such as *calm, relax, still,* or *peaceful.* Choose one word you like, and with each inhalation and exhalation, breathe the soothing word into your heart, and then breathe it out. Imagine the calming word flowing into and out from your heart with each breath. You might also imagine the word has a soothing, calm color.

3. **HEART CENTRED BREATHING:** Continue to breathe in this heart-centered way for at least two minutes as you continue to sustain a genuine feeling of appreciation or care.

I recommend practicing Heart Centered Breathing at least once a day. This is another technique you can practice anytime, anywhere.

You can discover many more, HMI tools and techniques by visiting their website: www.heartmath.org/resources/heartmath-tools/

Afterword

You can dramatically improve the overall quality of your life
far faster than you might think possible.
All you need is the desire to change, the decision to take action,
the discipline to practice the new behaviors you have chosen,
and the determination to persist until you get the results you want.
– Brian Tracy, Bestselling Author and Speaker

At the start of this book, I explained what anxiety is and how we create it. This knowledge is powerful, because once we understand anxiety is something we can control, it empowers us and puts us back in the driving seat. We can begin to be proactive in controlling our day-to-day anxiety.

The seven techniques contained in this book will help you to begin to regain control over your day-to-day anxiety. However, to be effective you need to use them consistently, and I encourage you to practice them to the point where they have become new habits.

As we are all unique, there is no one size fits all solution for anxiety and I invite you to discover the technique(s) most beneficial for you.

You may also choose to use these seven techniques in combination with some of these proven coping mechanisms:

- Exercise. Regular exercise is an integral part of dealing with, and preventing, anxiety symptoms. Physical exercise helps burn off the surplus energy created by activating the stress response.
- Deep relaxation exercises. Deep relaxation is the exact opposite of tension which means when you practice relaxation on a regular basis many of your anxiety symptoms will disappear. Deep relaxation is not achieved by just 'putting your feet up' but by learning proper muscle relaxation and then practicing it regularly. Deep relaxation should not only be used when experiencing anxiety symptoms but should become a regular part of everyday life as a prevention mechanism.
- Guided visualization
- Meditation/mindfulness exercises
- Yoga
- Tai Chi
- Massage

References & Suggested Reading

Boyes, Alice. (2015) *The Anxiety Toolkit.* New York: Penguin

Elliott, Charles H; Smith, Laura L. (2010) *Overcoming Anxiety for Dummies.* New Jersey: Wiley Publishing Inc

Griffin, Joe; Tyrell Ivan. (2011) *How to Master Anxiety.* Great Britain: HG Publishers

Horscroft, Alistair. (2013) *Beat Anxiety Now.* Kindle Edition

Human Givens College. (2015) *Understanding Anxiety and Managing it without Drugs.* Webinar.

Kabat-Zinn, Jon. (2005) *Full Catastrophe Living – Using the Wisdom of Your Body and Mind to Face Stress, Pain and Illness.* New York: Bantam Dell

Leahy, Robert L. (2005) *The Worry Cure: Seven Steps to Stop Worry from Stopping You.* Listen & Live Audio, Inc

McDonagh, Barry. (2015) *DARE – The New Way to End Anxiety and Stop Panic Attacks Fast.* Kindle Edition

McGonigal, Kelly. (2015) *The Upside of Stress: Why Stress Is Good for you, and How to Get Good at It.* London: Vermilion

Tiers, Melissa. (2011) *The Anti-Anxiety Toolkit.* Createspace

About the Author – Tony Yuile

Tony Yuile is a certified life coach, registered clinical hypnotherapist and NLP Master Practitioner. He lives in Wellington, New Zealand.

Tony is passionate about helping people develop the life skills they need to perform at their best under pressure, minimize the stress and anxiety in their lives and enhance their resilience. The outcome for his clients is they enjoy more success, happiness and a greater feeling of wellbeing.

Prior to life coaching, Tony spent 30 years in the corporate world as an accountant and a risk management specialist. He was secure and happy in his career until thrown a curve ball – redundancy, something he was totally unprepared for. Suddenly he found himself in the vicious grip of anxiety and stress.

When he finally emerged from beneath the black cloud, he promised himself he would never feel so dreadful again and set out to discover as much as he could about stress and anxiety. He spent three years studying modern psychology. Wanting to share what he'd learned with others, he trained to be a life coach. He has developed a solution-focused approach based on proven, practical, evidence-based strategies and techniques. Tony no longer spends his days balancing numbers, preferring instead to help people achieve balance and greater fulfilment in their lives.

Tony's specialties –

- Performing under pressure
- Anxiety management
- Stress management
- Resilience building
- Lifting depression
- Relieving trauma
- Overcoming phobias and irrational fears

Tony works with clients face to face and anywhere in the world via SKYPE.

If you are interested in exploring how Tony can help you perform your best under pressure and master your anxiety and stress, contact him at info@tycoaching.nz or via his website www.tycoaching.nz

CPSIA information can be obtained
at www.ICGtesting.com
Printed in the USA
LVHW051113010222
709871LV00016B/2767